LEBRON J

THE BIOGRAPHY

Richard Miller

CONTENTS

Introduction

LeBron James turned into a prompt star subsequent to skipping school to join the NBA's Cleveland Cavaliers. In 2012 and 2013, he led the Miami Heat to NBA championships. In 2016, he led Cleveland to another championship, and in 2018 he joined the Los Angeles Lakers.

Who's LeBron James?

American basketball player LeBron James plays for the Los Angeles Lakers. As the nation's best high school basketball player, James first attracted national attention. He won the NBA MVP four times thanks to his distinctive combination of size, athleticism, and court vision. James returned to Cleveland after leading the Miami Heat to titles in 2012 and 2013, where he helped the team win its first championship in 2016.

James was born in Akron, Ohio, on December 30, 1984. James demonstrated a natural talent for basketball at a young age. St. Vincent recruited him. During his four years there, James finished with 2,657 points, 892 rebounds, and 523 assists.

James scored an average of 18 points per game as a freshman. By scoring 25 points in the championship game, he helped the team win the Division III state championship. James received numerous awards for his performance as word of his advanced basketball skills spread.

James was named to the USA Today All-America First Team when he was a sophomore in high school. He was the only sophomore to ever receive this honor. Additionally, for the second year in a row, his team won the Division III state championship.

James won the Gatorade Player of the Year award and the High School Boys Basketball Player of the Year award from PARADE magazine during the subsequent academic year. Following the finish of his lesser year, James was such areas of strength that he considered going genius.

James had a fantastic senior year on the court as a result of his decision to finish his education. He contributed to his team's third state championship by scoring 31.6 points per game. One of the best players in the National Basketball Association would soon be

James Lebron.

How he was drafted:

James's selection as the first high school graduate in the 2003 NBA Draft came as no surprise given his impressive record. The powerful young forward was signed by the Cleveland Cavaliers, a struggling team at the time, and he proved to be a valuable addition. The previous campaign had seen the team finish eighth in the Eastern Conference.

During the 2003-2004 seasons, James became the first Cavalier player to win the NBA Rookie of the Year Award, making history. He was also the youngest player to receive this honor, at just 20 years old.

Additionally, James, who was scoring 20 points per game at the time, joined Oscar Robertson and Michael Jordan as the only rookies to accomplish this feat.

The following season, James continued to excel professionally in the NBA, averaging 27.2 points per game. In 2005, he remade NBA history by becoming the youngest player to score more than 50 points in a single game.

In the first round of the playoffs in 2006, James helped his team defeat the Washington Wizards. In the Eastern Conference semifinals, the Cavaliers faced the Detroit Pistons from that point on. In this playoff matchup, James scored an average of 26.6 points per game, but his team didn't win. James continued to receive special praise for his abilities even though his team did not rank highly.

James signed a new contract with the Cavaliers in 2006. The following season, the team defeated Detroit to win the Eastern Conference and demonstrated that they were stronger competitors. The Cavaliers, on the other hand, lost four games in a row to the San Antonio Spurs in the NBA Finals.

James continued to assist the Cavaliers in elevating their position in the Eastern Conference during the 2007–08 seasons. The Boston Celtics defeated the team in seven games to advance to the semifinals. In terms of individual performance, James had a stellar year.

He scored an average of 30 points per game, which was the highest average in the NBA regular season, beating out rival players like Kobe Bryant and Allen Iverson.

Sports journalists and fans began discussing James' future in the sport at the beginning of the 2008-09 seasons. In 2010, he could choose to become a free agent, and there was a lot of talk about where James would end up.

The young player's potential suitor, according to some journalists, could be the New York Knicks.

James made a few mentions of his upcoming free-agent status, but he always tried to downplay it. I'm centered around the group that I am on the present moment and coming out on top for a title ... I don't ponder rolling out an improvement as of now, "James told correspondents.

Miami Heat Career:

James made the announcement that he would be joining the Miami Heat for the 2010–11 seasons shortly after becoming a free agent. Many Cleveland fans saw his departure as a betrayal to his hometown, and they were not pleased.

Dan Gilbert, majority owner of the Cleveland Cavaliers, wrote an open letter shortly after James made his decision, calling it "selfish,""heartless," and a "cowardly betrayal."James managed to score 26.7 points per game and finish second in the league in his first season with the Heat.

James and the Miami Heat enjoyed significant success during the 2011–12 seasons. The superstar forward finally won his first title when his team beat the Oklahoma City Thunder in the NBA Finals. James had 26 points, 11 rebounds, and 13 assists in Game 5's decisive win. After the game, James told FOX Sports, "I made a difficult decision to leave Cleveland, but I understood what my future was about."In Miami, I was aware that we had a bright future.

James once more made NBA history in the 2012-13 seasons: He became the 38th player in NBA history to score 20,000 points on January 16, 2013, when he was 28 years old. He succeeded Bryant of the Lakers, who had done so when he was 29 years old, as the youngest player to do so. James scored 20,001 points with a jump shot in the final seconds of the game, leading the Heat to a 92-75 victory over the Warriors.

The Heat was successful until the end of the 2012–13 seasons: Miami defeated the San Antonio Spurs in seven games to win its second NBA championship in a row after a hard-fought six-game series to win the Eastern Conference.

At the end of the 2013-14 seasons, Miami went back to the NBA Finals to play the Spurs. This time, San Antonio won five games, and Miami lost.

Returning to the Cleveland Cavaliers

James announced in July 2014 that he would be returning to the Cavaliers after opting out of his contract with the Miami Heat and considering other teams.

Hampered by back and knee issues, James missed 13 of 82 ordinary season games in 2014-15. But when he was healthy, he was just as good as ever, scoring 25.3 points and dishing out 7.4 assists per game. James led the Cavaliers to the NBA Finals, making him the first player in nearly 50 years to do so five times in a row.

However, the Cavaliers' chances of winning a third title were harmed by injuries to star teammates Kyrie Irving and Kevin Love, and the team lost to the Golden State Warriors in six games.
Over the course of 2015-16, the Cavaliers overcame the distraction of a coaching change in the middle of the season and breezed through the playoffs to face the Warriors once more, making it 'King James' sixth consecutive NBA Finals appearance.

He led his team back from a 3-1 deficit in both Games 5 and 6, scoring 41 points in each, before putting up a triple-double in Game 7 to win the Cavaliers their first championship in franchise history.
James, who was awarded the Finals MVP, stated, "I came back to bring a championship to our city."I was aware of my capabilities. I knew I was gone because of what I had learned over the past few years, and if I had to return, I knew I had the right ingredients and the right plan to help this franchise get back to a place we've never been. That was the focus of everything.

The following year, James drove the Cavaliers through the Eastern Conference to an incredible seventh consecutive appearance in the NBA Finals while maintaining his own pace and taking charge when necessary.

The Warriors outlasted James and his team this time, adding former MVP Kevin Durant to the mix, winning the championship in five games.

James accomplished yet another first early in the 2017-18 NBA season, despite all of his accomplishments: He was kicked out for the first time in 1,082 games after yelling at a referee in a win over the Heat in late November.

As an unsuccessful offseason trade that would have sent Irving to Boston in exchange for Isaiah Thomas compelled the Cavaliers to make another significant deal before the All-Star break, the superstar probably felt the need to yell frequently throughout the course of a frustrating season.

James had a career-high 9.1 assists in the regular season, but he had to work hard to get the team out of the first round of the playoffs. In Game 7, he scored 45 points to beat the Pacers. James scored 81 points in the final two games to win the series and advance to the NBA Finals for the eighth time in his career. The Cavaliers were once more pushed to their limits by the competitive Celtics two rounds later.

Cleveland guard J.R. Smith inexplicably dribbled out the clock with the game tied in regulation before the Warriors pulled away for the win in overtime. Game 1 of the rematch against Golden State went down to the wire thanks to James's 51-point outburst, but the Warriors pulled away for the win in overtime. That was the Cavaliers' best chance to get ahead of their opponents, but the Warriors went on to win the next three games easily to win their third championship in four years.

James revealed that he had played out the series with a broken right hand after punching a whiteboard in the aftermath of the loss in Game 1, prompting questions about his future with the team.

LeBron James signs for the Lakers

On July 1, 2018, James signed a four-year, $153.3 million contract with the Los Angeles Lakers, a legendary team that boasts Bryant, Kareem Abdul-Jabbar, and Magic Johnson among its all-time greats. This move marked James' transition to the next phase of his career.

By the middle of the season, the Lakers had lost 17 games without their injured star, so the good vibes had faded.
"If you're still allowing distractions to affect the way you play, this is the wrong franchise to be a part of and you should just come in and be like, 'Listen, I can't do this, 'James said as the team continued to struggle in late February 2019.

James' personal record of 13 consecutive postseasons and eight consecutive NBA Finals appearances was broken when the Lakers were officially eliminated from playoff contention in March 2019. The Lakers announced that their star would miss the final six games of his first difficult season in Los Angeles due to a lingering injury to his groin.

The addition of athletic big man Anthony Davis to the roster was largely responsible for the improved start to the subsequent season. James was a driving force behind the Lakers' rise to the top of the standings. In November 2019, he became the first player to score a triple-double against all 30 NBA teams.

James was named AP Male Athlete of the Decade the following month, adding yet another honor to his ever-expanding list.
From the 2010-11 seasons through the 2018-19 seasons, James was a part of eight consecutive NBA championships. He won three championship rings in that time: once with the Cavaliers (2015-16) and twice with the Heat (2011-12 and 2012-13).

MVPs and All-Star Games James was selected for the first time for the NBA All-Star Game in 2005, and he would go on to participate in the annual competition in each of the subsequent 15 seasons.

The NBA announced in January 2018 that James and Golden State Warriors guard Stephen Curry had won the most votes and would be captains of the All-Star Game that year.

In 2006, James was named the Most Important Player in the NBA Top pick Game, an accomplishment he would rehash in 2008 and 2018. Additionally, James has won the NBA MVP award four times, in the years 2008-09, 2009-10, 2011-12, and 2012-13.
He has been named an all star 19 times.

Statistics and Points In January of 2018, James, then 33, became the seventh player in NBA history to surpass Bryant as the youngest player to score 30,000 points in a career. He was just over 8,000 points away from beating Abdul-Jabbar's all-time record of 38,387 points thanks to this achievement.

James surpassed Michael Jordan's career total of 32,292 points in 2019 to move up to fourth place on the list. He surpassed Bryant's 33,643 points in January 2020, one night before his predecessor's shocking death in a helicopter accident, to move into third place.
James had the following regular-season per-game averages after 16 NBA seasons:

27.2 points in 38.6 minutes, 0.736 free throw percentage, 0.343 field goal percentage from three, 0.504 field goal percentage, 1.2 offensive rebounds, 6.2 defensive rebounds, 7.2 assists, 0.8 blocks, 1.6 steals, and 3.5 turnovers.

LeBron James currently holds the record for most points scored by an NBA player.

In the Los Angeles Lakers' defeat to the Oklahoma City Thunder on February 7, the 38-year-old surpassed Kareem Abdul-Jabbar's previous record of 38,387 points.

'King James' a fitting moniker for a player, has won the most prestigious and recent award in his glittering career.
He continues to have a significant influence on the basketball

game.

Olympics participation

James represented the United States in basketball at three Summer Olympics—in 2004, 2008, and 2012.

At the Summer Games in Athens, Greece, in 2004, James made his Olympic debut. He and his teammates defeated Lithuania and won bronze medals. After defeating Italy in the finals, Argentina won the gold medal.

James went to Beijing, China, in the summer of 2008, to play on the U.S. Olympic basketball team with players like Bryant, Jason Kidd, and Dwyane Wade. The U.S. team won the gold this time around after defeating Spain in the final round.

Along with Durant, Bryant, Carmelo Anthony, and a number of other top players, James participated in his third Olympic Games, the Summer Olympics in London, in 2012. James won his second Olympic gold medal in a row for the U.S. basketball team.

Contracts:

In 2003, James signed a number of endorsement deals, one of which offered him $90 million and the potential to earn over $1 billion in his lifetime.

Beats by Dre, Intel, Verizon, Coca-Cola, and Kia Motors are among the other endorsements.

Salary and Earnings:

During the 2016–17 season, James made $31 million, making him the third player after Jordan and Bryant to earn that much.

In July 2018, the NBA superstar agreed to a $153.3 million, four-year deal with the Lakers.

He has also invested in Blaze Pizza and is a co-owner of the production company Spring Hill Entertainment.

Forbes magazine estimated James' annual earnings in February 2019 at $88.7 million, making him the NBA's highest-earning player for the fifth consecutive year.

Family

James proposed to Savannah Brinson, his high school sweetheart, on January 1, 2012. On September 14, 2013, the couple tied the knot in a private ceremony attended by approximately 200 people in San Diego.

Together, James and Brinson have two sons and a daughter. James gave birth to their first child, LeBron Jr., in October 2004. On June 14, 2007, Brinson gave birth to their second child, Bryce Maximus James. Zhuri James, their third child, was born on October 22, 2014.

LeBron James Family Foundation James has contributed to the welfare of others outside of the NBA. In order to assist children and single-parent families in need, he and his mother Gloria founded the LeBron James Family Foundation in 2004.

The organization organizes an annual bike-a-thon and builds playgrounds in economically disadvantaged areas as two of its many programs.
Posts that are outspoken on Social Media James, one of the most well-known athletes in the world, has never been afraid to say what he thinks on social media. He has argued with U.S. President Donald Trump and shown his support for Trayvon Martin following the teen's 2012 death.

In October 2019, Daryl Morey, the general manager of the Houston Rockets, sent a tweet in support of Hong Kong's pro-democracy protesters, which sparked a Chinese media boycott of NBA preseason games in China. This put James in delicate territory. James stated that he thought Morey was "misinformed" about the situation, but he later tweeted that he mostly disagreed with the executive's comments that could have put traveling players in danger.

The movie "Space Jam 2"

During the Cavaliers' slow start to the 2017-18 seasons, the superstar basketball player has also displayed a playful side on social media, such as when he posted a picture of the cartoon character Arthur clenching his first.

James starred in the 2021 sequel to the 1996 smash "Space Jam 2," which starred Jordan. James stated to The Hollywood Reporter, "The Space Jam collaboration is so much more than just me and the Looney Tunes working together on this movie".

It is enormously larger. I just want children to know how empowered they can feel and become if they don't give up on their dreams.

Facts about LeBron James:

After LeBron James left college to play for the Cleveland Cavaliers of the NBA, he became a household name right away. In 2012 and 2013, he led the Miami Heat to NBA championships. In 2016, he led Cleveland to another championship, and in 2018 he joined the Los Angeles Lakers.

LeBron James became the youngest NBA player to ever win the Rookie of the season, making him the first Cavaliers player of the Year Award during the 2003-2004 to do so.
During the 2003-2004 season, LeBron James was one of only three rookies to average 20 points per game. Oscar Robertson and Michael Jordan were the other rookies to do so.

LeBron James Quote:

"Although it was a difficult choice to leave Cleveland, I knew what my future would entail and that we would have a bright future in Miami".

"I never put things off until later. I'm going to attack. I will continue to play my game regardless of the number of weapons we have on the court".

"I was able to stay away from drugs and gangs thanks to sports. My exit was sports".

"Money is not the issue. For me, it's all about winning".

"When I say that I won't go to college, I never feel sad. However, I do wish I had been able to participate in March Madness".

"I'm a basketball fanatic".

"Each of our preparations is unique, but there is only one basketball on that court".

"We were aware that it would not be simple. It wasn't going to be simple for us. Numerous teams have easily won gold. That was not what we wanted".

"Because it is impossible, I do not evaluate my career by saying that I want to be better than this or that person at the end of it".

"I am the only one in and out of the court who must be satisfied".

"Just by being LeBron, LeBron maintains his modesty".

"Why would you think he will return? Every day, people move from Cleveland to Miami. They do not relocate to Cleveland from Miami".

The end.

Printed in Great Britain
by Amazon

33296409R00015